PUFFIN  LITTLE

Little
Historian

PUFFIN BOOKS

UK | USA | Canada | Ireland | Australia
India | New Zealand | South Africa | China

 Penguin
Random House
Australia

Penguin Random House Australia is part of the Penguin Random House group of companies
whose addresses can be found at global.penguinrandomhouse.com.

First published by Puffin Books, an imprint of Penguin Random House Australia Pty Ltd, in 2020

Printed in Singapore

 A catalogue record for this
book is available from the
NATIONAL
LIBRARY   National Library of Australia
OF AUSTRALIA

ISBN 978 1 76 089702 4

Penguin Random House Australia uses papers that are natural and recyclable products,
made from wood grown in sustainable forests. The logging and manufacture processes are
expected to conform to the environmental regulations of the country of origin.

penguin.com.au

PUFFIN LITTLE

The ANZACs

PUFFIN BOOKS

CONTENTS

HELLO, LITTLE HISTORIANS

WELCOME TO MY STUDY...

I'm so pleased you stopped by because today we are going to learn about some very important men and women from Australian history . . .

The Australian and New Zealand Army Corps – **The ANZACs!**

On **Anzac Day**, 25 April each year, we remember the men and women who have served our country in times of war.

You might have heard Big Historians talking about the Anzacs, but do you know who the Anzacs were and what they did?

To find out, we need to go back over one hundred years, to where it all began.

It started with our involvement in World War I, when Britain and Germany went to war in 1914.

We might be LITTLE, but we've got some **BIG** facts to learn.

Are you ready?

Then turn the page . . .

1914: THE OUTBREAK OF WAR

World War I was a global conflict that took place between 1914 and 1918.

It was fought mainly in Europe, but it also spread to the Middle East, Africa and Asia.

This war was different to all the other wars fought before because huge numbers of people were involved. Soldiers fought and died in their millions.

But how did it start?

Well, Little Historians, it started with a gun shot ...

On 28 June 1914, **Archduke Franz Ferdinand**, the heir to the throne of Austria-Hungary, and his wife Sophie were shot and killed by a Serbian called **Gavrilo Princip** in the Balkan city of Sarajevo.

Because its leader had been shot, Austria-Hungary declared war on Serbia one month later on **28** July. As a result:

① **30 July:** Russia became involved through their alliance with Serbia

② **3 August:** Germany declared war on Russia because of their alliance with Austria-Hungary

③ **4 August:** Britain declared war on Germany because of their agreement to protect neutral Belgium and France

Within a week, most of Europe was at war.

This is all very confusing isn't it,

Little Historians?

To understand exactly why these countries got

involved, we need to learn about **ALLIANCES**.

Let's find out!
Left, right,
left, right . . .

ALLIANCE

An alliance is a special relationship between countries.

They agree to protect each other. If one gets attacked, the other will defend them.

Members of an alliance are called allies.

When we think back to the outbreak of World War I, we can now understand why these countries got involved.

By 4 August 1914, the world was at war, and the war was being fought between two groups, **The Allies** and **The Central Powers**.

The Allies (also known as **The Triple Entente**) was the name given to the alliance between **Russia**, **France** and **Britain**.

The Central Powers was the name given to **Germany**, **Austria-Hungary** and **their supporters**.

You might still be wondering how a war between just a handful of countries can be called a **WORLD WAR** . . .

The answer, Little Historians, is **EMPIRE**.

EMPIRE

An EMPIRE is a group of countries (colonies) ruled over by a single monarch or ruling power.

In 1914, Great Britain, Germany, Austria-Hungary, Italy and Russia all ruled huge empires, stretching across the world.

With the outbreak of war, each colony sent supplies, food and soldiers to help their empire in the war effort.

But what has this got to do with the Anzacs?

Well, Little Historians, at the time of World War I, Australia and New Zealand were part of the **British Empire**.

When the British government called on them for support, they were keen to do all they could to help the **mother country**. Ultimately, their greatest contribution to the war effort was the supply of soldiers.

THE BRITISH EMPIRE

Britain's colonies sent over two and a half million men to fight for the Allies in the war.

Along with Australia and New Zealand, British colonies as far away as India, Canada, South Africa and Rhodesia (which is now Zimbabwe) sent thousands of soldiers.

That meant that Britain had soldiers from five different continents: **Europe**, **North America**, **Australia**, **Asia** and **Africa**.

DID YOU KNOW...

In 1914, 400 million people – one quarter of the world – lived in the British Empire.

How many soldiers from the British Empire served?

Britain	5,000,000
India	1,440,437
Canada	628,964
Australia	412,953
South Africa	136,070
New Zealand	128,825
Other colonies	134,837

Most of the fighting happened in Europe, but now we know all about empire and colonies, it's clear to see how the war affected people from all over the world.

Now you can see why they called it a World War!

The Allies

The Central Powers

MEET THE ANZACS

Australia and New Zealand received word of Britain's declaration of war on 5 August 1914. Within a matter of days, thousands of Australians and New Zealanders were volunteering to fight.

But why did so many young men and women want to fight in a war so far from home?

Let's take a look at some of the reasons . . .

EMPIRE

Australia and New Zealand were part of the British Empire. They were **loyal** to Britain and saw the empire's enemies as their own.

Many Australians and New Zealanders also thought of themselves as British and of Britain as home, so they wanted to help the mother country in its moment of crisis.

Andrew Fisher, the leader of the Labor Party at the time, said:

Australians will stand beside the mother country to help and defend her to our last man and our last shilling.

DUTY

A lot of young volunteers thought it was their duty to **do the right thing**.

They believed in the war and didn't just want to support the empire, they also wanted to fight the 'cruel' and 'savage' enemy.

During the beginning of the war, news of the awful actions committed by the Central Powers convinced many to hate these enemy nations, such as Germany.

AUSTRALIANS! YOUR COUNTRY NEEDS YOU.

EXPECTATION

A lot of pressure was put on young men to volunteer. It was expected of them, and they didn't want to let their communities down.

By signing up for the war, they were proving themselves to be **fit**, **strong** and **capable**.

ADVENTURE

Many young Australians and New Zealanders had never travelled beyond their state, let alone overseas. When the war arrived, it was seen as an opportunity to reach faraway lands and experience adventure.

At the start of the war, no one really knew how terrible it would be. In fact, many people thought it would only last a few weeks! They had no idea it would go on for **four devastating years**.

FRIENDS

A lot of young men signed up to go to war because their friends did. There was also the worry that if they didn't volunteer, their friends would think they were **cowards**.

A WHITE FEATHER

The Order of the White Feather was a way to encourage women to pressure their family and friends into enlisting for the war.

White feathers were given to young, fit men who did not volunteer for service, labelling them as cowards. That seems pretty mean, don't you think?!

MONEY

Australian soldiers received a wage of six shillings a day. This was a lot of money compared to other jobs at home.

Volunteering for the war meant they would get paid regularly and on time. A very attractive reason for many young men to join the war.

Australian troops were sometimes called 'six bob a day tourists' in reference to their wage.

As you can see, Little Historians, there were lots of reasons why so many people volunteered to fight in the war.

BECOMING THE ANZACS

By October 1914, over 20,000 Australians had joined the **Australian Imperial Force (AIF)**, and 8000 New Zealanders had joined the **New Zealand Expeditionary Force (NZEF)**.

In December 1914, the AIF and NZEF went off to train for war under the command of **Lieutenant General William Birdwood**. Initially, the term **Australasian Corps** was suggested for the two forces, but Australians and New Zealanders didn't want to lose their separate identities completely.

The soldiers in the AIF and NZEF quickly became known as **The ANZACs**.

The word represents the shared heritage of two nations, but it also has a specific meaning – **The Australian and New Zealand Army Corps**. No one knows for sure who came up with ANZAC. It is likely that a clerk at Birdwood's headquarters thought of it to use on a rubber stamp: 'ANZAC' was convenient shorthand.

WHAT IS A DIGGER?

The Anzac soldiers were also called DIGGERS.

In Australia, after World War I, 'digger' became the nickname for the veterans who had returned home.

AN EGYPTIAN ADVENTURE

The fresh volunteer troops from Australia and New Zealand were excited to set off to England for **training**. But with overcrowding and shortages of equipment at the British training camps, it was decided the Anzacs had to start their war adventure in a different land.

Instead of the lush green fields of England, the wide-eyed young men found themselves in the desert heat of **Egypt**. They made their home at **Mena Camp**, a huge training camp in the shadow of the famous Sphinx and pyramids of Giza.

The promise of a wartime adventure and exploring foreign lands seemed to be coming true. Most of the young diggers had never before left Australia, let alone the Southern Hemisphere.

After travelling for eight long weeks by ship, the Anzacs got to work setting up Mena Camp.

Thousands of men lived, worked and trained there in a city of tents and barracks.

Soldiers also wrote home about the leisure time they enjoyed, visiting the **pyramids** and places named in the Bible. With their wages in their pockets, many took tours of the tombs and haggled with Egyptian traders for souvenirs in the markets of Cairo, sending precious keepsakes home to their families.

One digger wrote to his family about Mena Camp, on 14 December 1915:

We are camped in the Valley of the Pyramids with two of the big Pyramids in sight. They are an enormous size – a wonderful piece of work ... The camp is like a huge town. We have been making rifle ranges, building latrines, making roads, building mess rooms and a thousand and one jobs which are required in a big camp like this.

However, it wasn't all fun and games, it was tough at Mena Camp. For **eight hours a day, six days a week**, the Anzacs trained for war.

Early every morning the soldiers paraded in full kits and backpacks and trudged through kilometres of sandy desert. Many became ill with **heatstroke** as they trained on the desert sand. A few even died of **pneumonia** because of the freezing winter nights.

**Private George Plows from Dunedoo NSW,
wrote home telling his family about his
daily routine:**

*We get up at 6am and have breakfast (or a slice of
bread and butter and a cup of tea), and at 7am we
go for a six hours' march across the desert, in sand
up to our ankles. We have dinner at 3pm and tea
at 6.30, and often have to do a two hours' march at
night. It is winter here now, and the nights are very
cold. It is fairly hot in the daytime. It is deadly when
you look around and can only see sand for miles.*

DIGGER MASCOTS

After all the excitement of travelling to faraway lands and building the camp below the pyramids, the reality of just how far away from home they were must have made the Anzac diggers feel very homesick. Luckily, there were a few **digger mascots** hopping around camp who made the soldiers feel right at home . . .

Australian animals such as kangaroos, kookaburras, koalas and other species were smuggled on board the transport ships that carried Australian troops to Egypt.

The kangaroos and wallabies in the Anzac camps served a more important purpose than just a reminder of home – they became **digger mascots**.

As the months dragged on at the training camps, maintaining high spirits was essential. The presence of a kangaroo or wallaby helped to keep Anzac troops as happy as possible under the circumstances.

When the troops left the training camps the animals were donated to the Cairo Zoological Gardens where they lived out the rest of their lives in peace.

OFF TO THE FRONT

After four months of training in Egypt, the Anzacs were keen to get to war.

On 1 April 1915, the men finally got their wish and were ordered to the **front line**.

The Anzacs were being sent to a place in Turkey called **Gallipoli**.

FRONT LINE

The front line was the point where the armies of each side met. This was where most of the fighting took place.

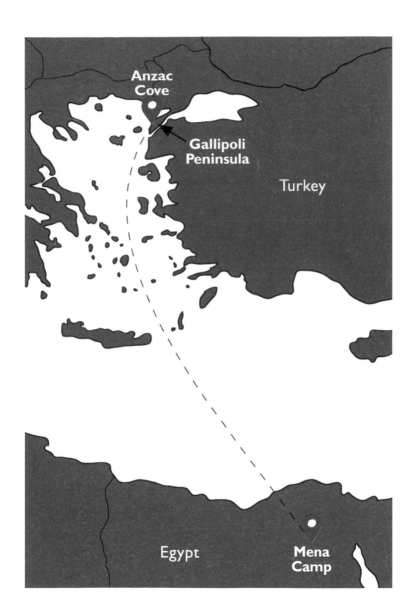

Anzac
Cove

Gallipoli
Peninsula

Turkey

Egypt

Mena
Camp

GALLIPOLI

We have learnt lots of fascinating facts about the Anzacs and their wartime adventure so far. Now we're going to learn about the battle that is at the heart of the **Anzac legend**.

The Gallipoli Campaign.

It was here that the Anzacs showed their tireless endurance, strength and courage in times of struggle.

WHY GALLIPOLI?

The **Ottoman Empire** was part of the **Central Powers** alliance, together with Germany and Austria-Hungary. It controlled the Turkish waterway that connects the **Mediterranean Sea** with the **Black Sea,** an area called the **Dardanelles**.

With the Dardanelles under the control of the Central Powers, Russia, who was part of **The Allies,** could not get any important supplies by sea because the Central Powers kept blocking the way.

The Allies' plan was to attack **Gallipoli**, knock **Turkey** out of the war and take power of the **Dardanelles**.

What was thought to be a simple operation, turned out to be anything but.

THE
MEDITERRANEAN
SEA

Anzac
Cove

TO THE
BLACK SEA

The Dardanelles

GALLIPOLI

THE LANDING

In the early hours of **25 April 1915**, the Anzacs landed on Turkey's **Gallipoli Peninsula** at a place we now know as **Anzac Cove**.

The soldiers were nervous, a long way from home, ready to rush ashore and fight. Their mission was to beat the Turkish army and quickly win the war.

But what happened, Little Historians, was very different . . .

In darkness, they faced a tough and difficult climb up the beach. The Anzacs had to get past high cliffs, steep ridges, deep gullies and thick scrub, while from above, Turkish soldiers fired on them.

The new army of Anzacs were at a big disadvantage, and they were up against tough and experienced Turkish soldiers who were prepared to give their lives to defend their homeland.

The first day of the battle was a disaster. Over 2000 Anzacs lost their lives and countless were wounded.

But this was just the start of what was to be **eight months** of conflict and loss.

TRENCH WARFARE

After the disastrous first day of fighting, the Anzacs
held strong and began to dig deep, narrow alleys
into the ground where they could escape the enemy
attack. This was called **trench warfare**.

The majority of battles that took place in World War I
used trench warfare. Both sides built deep trenches
as a defence against the enemy. The trenches were
dug by the soldiers and stretched for many kilometres,
making it nearly impossible for one side to advance.

The trenches were dug as deeply as possible so that
a soldier could safely stand up in them. It was still a
good idea to wear a helmet!

Soldiers were ordered to 'go over the top' and head into no-man's-land. Scary!

The ground between the two opposing trenches was called **no-man's-land**.

So, Little Historians, let's find out what life in the trenches was like for the Anzac diggers at Gallipoli …

LIFE IN THE TRENCHES

Life was not easy for the soldiers at Gallipoli. The battlefield was a horrible place for both the Anzacs and the Turks.

The trenches weren't just used to protect the soldiers when fighting. This maze of deep narrow alleys became their home.

The Anzacs were expected to dig out their own room in the side of the trenches. These were called **dug-outs**.

The trenches were not nice, clean places. They were actually very dirty. There were all sorts of pests living in the trenches including rats, lice and frogs. The rats were everywhere and got into the soldiers' food and ate just about everything, including nibbling on sleeping soldiers!

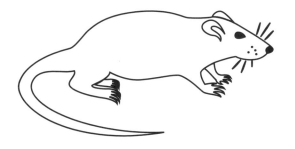

This extract from Corporal George L. Smith's poem, *My Anzac Home*, gives us an idea of what trench life was like at Gallipoli . . .

Come and see my little dug-out way up on the hill it stands.
Where I can get a lovely view of Anzac's golden sands;
When 'beach billy' is shelling, I can see just where it lands,
From my cosy little dug-out on the hill.

The fleas they wander nightly, as soon as I've undressed,
And after many weary hunts I've had to give them best.
As the ants have also found it, there is very little rest
In my cosy little dug-out on the hill.

I've a natty little cupboard, and it looks so very nice.

'Twas made to keep my bread and jam, my bacon and my rice;

But now it's nothing other than a home for orphaned mice.

In my cosy little dug-out on the hill.

When the time comes round for parting from my little eight by four,

And I get a good night's rest without a back that's sore,

Well – perhaps some day I'll miss you, and will long to live once more

In the little cosy dug-out on the hill.

Trench life doesn't sound very nice at all!

A DIGGER'S DIET

We all look forward to a wholesome and tasty meal after a long day at school, don't we, Little Historians? What do you think was on the menu for the Anzacs?

An average meal, after a tough day in the trenches, looked a bit like this: some **cheese**, some **jam** and **tea** and a very hard biscuit, known as **hardtack** or the **Anzac tile**. The highlight was some **bully beef** – this was tinned corned beef.

As you can see, there were no fresh fruits or vegetables for the Anzacs. These rations were intended to be lived on for only short periods of time, not for months and months as they had to at Gallipoli.

HARDTACK

Hardtack biscuits often broke a soldier's teeth. Sometimes the biscuits were grated or ground up to make porridge or to thicken a stew made with bully beef and onions.

This doesn't sound very appetising.

Sing me to sleep, the bullets fall
Let me forget the war and all
Damp is my dug-out, cold is my feet
Nothing but biscuits and bully to eat.

          – popular soldier's song

CARING FOR THE SICK AND WOUNDED

Hundreds of men fell ill and were wounded in battle every day at Gallipoli.

Brave stretcher-bearers would carry wounded soldiers from the front line to safety where nurses and doctors would do all they could to care for them.

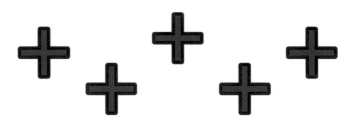

SIMPSON AND HIS DONKEY

Private John Simpson Kirkpatrick (or **Simpson** as he was known), was a stretcher-bearer in the Australian Army Medical Corps at Gallipoli.

Night and day, he rescued injured men from the front line and transported them to safety at Anzac Cove on the back of his donkey.

The donkey, called **Duffy,** had originally been brought to Gallipoli to carry water, but with Simpson, it found a much greater cause.

In only 24 days at Gallipoli, Simpson and his donkey rescued around 300 wounded soldiers.

There is a special statue of Simpson and his donkey at the Australian War Memorial in Canberra.

TOUGH TIMES

As the months of war dragged on, conditions in the trenches got worse and food rations dwindled. Life got harder and harder for the diggers, but one thing the Anzacs were famous for was their good humour and positivity in times of struggle.

On Gallipoli, a number of trench newspapers containing snippets of news, gossip and jokes made their way around the soldiers. These newspapers kept spirits high and allowed the men to share stories and experiences with their mates.

THE DINKUM OIL

One of the best-known newspapers was
The Dinkum Oil – this was slang for 'genuine
information'. These trench papers were an
important way in which the experiences of the
Anzac diggers has been shared and understood
as copies were sent home to families and
extracts were published in various newspapers.

Reading *The Dinkum Oil* today helps us
understand what life was like for the soldiers in
Gallipoli, and reveals not only the difficult and
dangerous experiences of the men but also their
good spirits and humour.

THE END OF A BLOODY BATTLE

For eight long months, the Anzacs and the Turks battled it out, with neither side gaining ground. By December 1915, over 11,000 Anzac soldiers had died. The Gallipoli Campaign had been a failure.

The Allies decided it was time to evacuate. But they needed a cunning plan to escape and avoid any more precious lives being lost during the evacuation.

Luckily, a plucky young Lance Corporal, **William Charles Scurry**, who had a passion for inventions, had a stroke of genius.

THE DRIP RIFLE

Scurry's invention, called the drip rifle, fooled the Turks into thinking a large force was still firing back at them, when in fact the rifles were shooting without anyone pulling the trigger. This enabled the soldiers to sneak away.

It worked by using two tin cans, one filled with water with a hole punched in it and the other empty and attached to the rifle's trigger using string.

The rifle was loaded and fixed in position with sandbags. Over time the water would drip out of the first can, filling the lower can until it had reached a certain weight, pulling the trigger and firing the weapon.

By dawn on the morning of 20 December, all the Anzacs were gone, with not a single man killed.

ANZAC LEGEND

Even though Gallipoli was just one small part of a much bigger conflict, and the Anzacs led other successful campaigns later in the war, we commemorate this battle because it was here that the Anzac legend was born.

Life on the battlefield and in the trenches was extremely hard at Gallipoli, but the Anzacs never gave up. In fact, the Anzacs were known as among the most fearsome and willing troops in the Allied forces. They made the best of an awful situation, showing courage, mateship and endurance, in the midst of fighting, hunger, flies, mud and death.

Anzac came to stand not only for the soldiers themselves, but also for the positive qualities they exhibited throughout the war, such as:

- ☆ **ENDURANCE**
- ☆ **COURAGE**
- ☆ **INGENUITY**
- ☆ **GOOD HUMOUR**
- ☆ **MATESHIP**

THE SLOUCH HAT

The Rising Sun badge, worn on the up-turned brim of a slouch hat, was a symbol of the spirit of the Anzacs – the mateship of Anzac soldiers to fight for the Crown, the mother country and the British Empire.

The slouch hat became an icon of Anzac bravery.

WOMEN & THE HOME FRONT

Women might not have fought on the front line with their Anzac brothers, but we should not forget the role they played in supporting the soldiers, both on the battlefield and at home.

Australian women volunteered for the war in any way they could: as cooks, nurses, drivers, interpreters, munitions operators and farm workers – everyone wanted to do their bit.

Their battles might have been different, but the Anzac spirit was the same.

WOMEN AT THE FRONT

NURSES

Women were allowed to serve in the army as nurses, but only if they were already trained.

Like the young men at the time, many women wanted to volunteer for the war. Nursing provided amazing opportunities for **independence** and **travel**, and sometimes it enabled them to be closer to loved ones serving overseas.

Over 3000 Australian and New Zealand nurses served in World War I and were instrumental in saving the lives of the diggers who made it through.

The women worked in hospitals, on hospital ships and trains, or at casualty points close to the front line where they were exposed to **shelling** and **bombs** as well as **outbreaks of disease**.

Just like the soldiers on the front line, the conditions the nurses worked in were hard and frightening. Despite these conditions, they carried on with courage and bravery, making them true Anzacs.

Not all women could volunteer to be nurses. Let's find out what some other women did to contribute!

Plenty of women made their mark in other roles on the **front line** throughout the war.

LOUISE MACK

JOURNALIST

Tasmanian-born Louise Mack was one of the first female war correspondents.

In 1914 when war broke out, Louise was in Belgium. Without fear, she reported on the German invasion for the *Evening News* and London's *Daily Mail*.

In 1917, she returned to Sydney and toured the country speaking about her experiences and raising money for the Australian Red Cross.

OLIVE KELSO KING

AMBULANCE DRIVER

In 1914, sydney-born Olive King was visiting England when the war broke out. Keen to 'do her bit' for the war effort, Olive served as an ambulance driver in Belgium. She converted a truck into a 16-seater ambulance, and later named it 'Ella the elephant'.

GLADYS SANDFORD

PIONEERING DRIVER

Gladys tried to enlist as a driver in the New Zealand Expeditionary Forces, but was turned down. Instead, she joined the New Zealand Volunteer Sisterhood and travelled to Egypt at her own cost in 1916, where she worked as an ambulance driver for a hospital in Giza. Later in the war, she was employed by the NZEF and promoted to head lady driver, serving in Egypt and France.

WOMEN AT HOME

Back in Australia and New Zealand on the home front, women took on the jobs previously done by men. This was a huge change for women. Before the war, many women had not worked outside the home. Along with their new duties, they had to take care of their young families or take on work with the Red Cross, raising funds for the troops.

Women invested a lot of emotional labour in the war effort by caring for the troops and sending comforts to the front. They knitted vests, scarves, mittens and socks; packed parcels; wrote letters; and became involved in fundraising for armaments and ambulances.

Women also dealt with the consequences of war – managing children and family responsibilities alone, shortages of resources such as food and clothing, as well as their fears for the future, and the grief of losing loved ones.

ANZAC BISCUITS

In an effort to raise money, women at home began to make the now famous ANZAC BISCUITS.

It has been said that these sweet treats were sent by wives and women's groups to soldiers at the front because the ingredients did not spoil easily, and the biscuits kept well during naval transportation.

ANZAC BISCUITS

Okay, Little Historians, we can't learn about the Anzacs without having a go at making some traditional Anzac biscuits!

This recipe was published in the Rockhampton newspaper *The Capricornian* on Saturday, 14 August 1926.

Ingredients

- ☆ 2 cups rolled oats
- ☆ ½ cup sugar
- ☆ 1 cup plain flour
- ☆ ½ cup melted butter
- ☆ 1 tbsp golden syrup
- ☆ 2 tbsp boiling water
- ☆ 1 tsp bicarbonate soda (add a little more water if mixture is too dry)

Method

1. Heat the oven to 160°C.

2. Combine dry ingredients.

3. Mix golden syrup, boiling water and bicarbonate of soda until they froth. Add melted butter.

4. Combine butter mixture and dry ingredients.

5. Drop teaspoons of mixture onto greased tray, allowing room for spreading.

6. Bake in the oven for 8–10 minutes until golden.

What do you think, Little Historians?

Aren't they delicious!

CHILDREN AT HOME

Children on the home front were keen to lend a hand and do their bit for the war effort.

The outbreak of war meant that family life was disrupted. Many men were off fighting in foreign lands, and women were encouraged to take up the jobs that were left behind. This meant a lot of children now found themselves with the job of looking after their younger brothers and sisters, helping with housework and preparing meals.

Some children helped to work the land by growing vegetables and collecting milk and eggs. Others contributed to fundraising efforts by collecting scrap metal, knitting socks and scarves and writing letters to soldiers.

But perhaps the hardest thing for children in World War I was waiting for news of family members from the front line.

DID YOU KNOW...

Some boys lied about their age and went off to fight. The age of enlistment in Australia was 21, or 18 if you had the written consent of your parents. But some boys as young as 14 found their way to the front lines!

ANZAC DAY

The date 25 April was officially named **Anzac Day** in 1916, a year after the young diggers landed on the beach at Gallipoli. The day was marked with ceremonies and services in Australia and New Zealand, a march through London and a sports day in the Australian camp in Egypt.

Nowadays, Anzac Day is a day when Australians and New Zealanders reflect on war. While Anzac Day was originally meant to honour the soldiers who fought and died at Gallipoli, it is now used to honour all soldiers who have fought and died for Australia and New Zealand.

THE DAWN SERVICE

**So, Little Historians, how do we
commemorate Anzac Day?**

In Australia and New Zealand, we start the Anzac
Day commemoration with a **Dawn Service**.

This tradition is symbolic of the dawn landing at
Gallipoli. Before dawn the gathered veterans are
ordered to 'stand-to' – this means to 'man their
positions'.

A single bugle (a brass horn instrument) plays the
Last Post. This is followed by one or two minutes
of silence to remember the fallen soldiers.

The Last Post was
originally played during
war to tell soldiers the day
was over. When the Last Post is
played at memorial services it
symbolises that the duty of the
dead is over and that they are
able to rest in peace.

At services today, we sing
hymns and read poems, and end
with a gun salute and **Reveille**
(the bugle call to wake up).

After the Dawn Service, Anzac Day parades are also held, with ex-servicemen and women marching in uniform.

Flowers and wreaths are laid on graves or memorials, and a **poppy** or **sprig of rosemary** is worn by veterans.

RED POPPIES

Poppies symbolise the bloodshed in war. After the war ended, red poppies were the first plants to grow on the devastated French and Belgian battlefields.

Soldiers used to say that their red colour came from all the blood spilt on the ground.

A SPRIG OF ROSEMARY

Have you ever wondered why rosemary is worn?

Rosemary has long featured in Anzac Day ceremonies, pinned to the jackets of servicemen and school children alike. The aromatic herb has a direct link with Gallipoli, where the Anzacs fought, and can be found growing wild all over the peninsula.

So now you know, Little Historians, tell your mates to pin a sprig on their jackets!

ANZAC DAY ACTIVITIES

As Little Historians, there are lots of things we can do to commemorate Anzac Day.

VISIT YOUR LOCAL WAR MEMORIAL

Most Australian towns have a monument to the local men who died, as well as parks, sports grounds and buildings named after battles, campaigns and heroes.

Take a trip to your local war memorial and look at the names engraved on the role of honour. Choose a name to research and see if someone in your community is able to tell you more about that person.

LOOK INTO YOUR FAMILY TREE

Perhaps a member of your family fought in World War I, or maybe someone volunteered to help the war effort at home.

Talk to older family members of your family and see if they have any stories to share.

So, Little Historians, on 25 April, take a moment and remember the **bravery** of the soldiers who fought on the battlefields of World War I, and the service of all those who have fought for their countries since then.

They shall grow not old,

As we that are left grow old,

Age shall not weary them,

Nor the years condemn.

At the going down of the sun,

And in the morning

We will remember them.

LEST WE FORGET.

– extract from 'For the Fallen'
by Laurence Binyon

NOT A HERO

Clyde Hamilton

The ANZAC Day march was over – the old Digger had done his best.

His body ached from marching – it was time to sit and rest.

He made his way to a park bench and sat with lowered head.

A young boy passing saw him – approached and politely said,

"Please sir do you mind if I ask you what the medals
you wear are for?
Did you get them for being a hero, when fighting in
a war?"
Startled, the old Digger moved over and beckoned
the boy to sit.
Eagerly the lad accepted – he had not expected this!
"First of all I was not a hero," said the old Digger in
solemn tone,
"But I served with many heroes, the ones that never
came home.
So when you talk of heroes, it's important to
understand,
The greatest of all heroes gave their lives defending
this land.

"The medals are worn in their honour, as a symbol
of respect.
All diggers wear them on ANZAC Day — it shows
they don't forget."
The old digger then climbed to his feet and asked
the boy to stand.
Carefully he removed the medals and placed them in
his hand.
He told him he could keep them — to treasure
throughout his life,
A legacy of a kind — left behind — paid for in
sacrifice.
Overwhelmed the young boy was speechless — he
couldn't find words to say.

It was there the old Digger left him — going quietly
on his way.

In the distance the young boy glimpsed him — saw
him turn and wave goodbye.

Saddened he sat alone on the bench — tears welled
in his eyes.

He never again saw him ever — but still remembers
with pride,

When the old Digger told him of Heroes and a
young boy sat and cried.

THE ANZACS IN WORLD WAR I

28 June

Archduke Franz
Ferdinand was
assassinated

4 August

Australians and
New Zealanders
volunteered to fight
for the mother
country

1 April

Diggers ordered
to the front line at
Gallipoli

1914	1915

28 July

Austria-Hungary
declared war on
Serbia –
World War 1 begins

1 October

Troops arrived at
training camps in
Egypt

25 April

ANZACs landed at
Anzac Cove

11 November

Armistice with

Germany signed –

World War 1 ends

20 December

Troops all

evacuated

1916	1917	1918	1919

25 April

Officially named

Anzac Day

28 June

Treaty of Versailles

signed

GLOSSARY

ALLIED POWERS: the alliance between Britain, France and Russia. The Allied Powers, also known as the Allies, fought against the Central Powers.

ANZAC: the name given to the soldiers serving with the Australian and New Zealand Army Corps (ANZAC).

BRITISH EMPIRE: the United Kingdom and the former territories under its control. Australia and New Zealand were part of the British Empire in 1914.

BULLY BEEF: tinned corned beef.

CASUALTY: a person who is injured or killed in war.

CENTRAL POWERS: the alliance between Germany and Austria-Hungary and their supporters. They fought against the Allied Powers.

DARDANELLES: the Turkish waterway that connects the Mediterranean and Black seas.

DAWN SERVICE: a ceremony held on 25 April, Anzac Day.

DIGGER: nickname for an Anzac soldier.

FRONT LINE: a place where two opposing military forces fight each other.

HARDTACK: a hard, flat biscuit that was included in the soldiers' rations.

HOME FRONT: the country where civilians live, supporting the troops.

NO-MAN'S-LAND: the area of land between the trenches that is not controlled by any side during a battle.

TRENCH WARFARE: a war where each side digs long lines of trenches for protection.

TROOPS: a group of soldiers.

VETERAN: a person who served in the armed forces for their country during a war.

PUFFIN QUIZ

1. Who was **assassinated** on 28 June 1914?

2. What does **ANZAC** stand for?

3. In which **country** did the Anzac troops train?

4. What **date** did the Anzacs land at Gallipoli?

5. What herb is worn in **remembrance** on Anzac Day?

A PUFFIN LITTLE BOOK